**poetry from author's blog:
www.theantifaux.blogspot.com

dedication

This is to the Queens who allowed me the space to grow and become the better me. To the Queens who loved my tear-stained face every time my smile went missing. To the Queens who let me bitch, moan and cry in text messages, on phone lines and on shoulders.
I stand tall, I stand whole, I stand HAPPY because of your love, support and much needed reality checks. I adore you all. I am grateful that I am now able to give to others what you all gave to me:

Love.

And to Julian, thank you for loving me in your own way so that I could learn to love myself in the right one.

xo,
MiaMcK

introduction

This has been buzzing around in my heart and spirit for the past twenty minutes. I tried stalling it, hoping to fall asleep, because church is in a couple of hours. But nope! The "better Mia" has been awakened and she won't let me continue to do the same ole thang aka the "run from greatness" dance, as I have come to call it. On most days, my actions (or inactions in this case) are reminiscent of the greatest two-step or shuffle that has ever graced any Soul Train line. Some days I refer to my moves as the "I have a good idea, but I allow fear to creep in before action takes place" dance. Then there's the "am I enough to pull this off?" dance I know all too well. And let's not even forget about the "oh well! It wouldn't have worked anyway" two-step. Have I reached your dance floor yet? While these dances won't be found as a tutorial on YouTube and are as played out as the Harlem Shake, the Macarena and the Running Man, they're very popular and real. As I lay here, piecing this together, I know that now is the right move. On most other days, the "so you think you can be great?" whispers would stall me. Today, I am realizing that it's going to shift a lot of mess for a number of Queens... especially myself. This book is for both of us. This is everything that I wish I'd had sense enough to apply. I would have spared myself the failures, the ego trips, the depression, the wilderness and the epic bouts with heartache caused by men not meant for me. We all go through the same things and I am now aware that we are never alone in our struggles.

So this...
this is To The Queens.

Poetically Inclined

Fair Weather

*I never realized I was so cold, until summer
came...
suddenly, I began to feel again.
and I didn't realize it hurt so badly,
until the tears wouldn't stop falling.
let's be honest, I've been addicted to the pain
you serve.
sick it seems, that the pain even felt good.
anything to feel connected,
to know that something still existed here.
like playing in the fallen leaves of autumn,
pleased to know beauty once flourished.
even if all that was left were barren branches.
unsure how it happened, but I'm grateful to be
free.
no dramatic exit.
simply decided to no longer exist to you
I've given me, wholly.
allowed you to invade my most amazing
spaces.
mind. body. heart. spirit.
it was you.*

to the core of me.
but I grew weary, pretending to be blind to
the vibrant colors.
hues that looked a lot like lies and deception,
ignored rainbows of wasted time and
disrespect.
all because I was obsessed with the rain.
passionate storms of you, left parts of me
absolutely damaged.
but I'm free.
and fairer weather is on the gloomy horizon.

xo,
McK

To the Queens: going through a break up

Breathe.

Yep, that is my first piece of advice. Why? Because I know how laborious breathing can feel when your heart is shattered. Taking a deep breath, after your heart has been reduced to nothing, feels like the body is birthing a goodbye. Imagine years or months of time, love, energy and memories have settled in the pit of your stomach; and the act of holding your breath seems to be the only way to control the floodgate of tears. It's as if exhaling will shock your body out of its numb state and the pain then becomes real again. I get it.

But, breathe.

Let that breath signify that there is still life in you. The break up, in fact, did not kill you.

Next, cry.
Cry and cleanse.

Don't believe the hype. This phase is supposed to hurt. Another myth that needs busting: crying is synonymous with being weak. This is simply not true. Your tears will be the very thing that waters the seeds of your growth. That's exactly what this is: the beginning of a new growth spurt.

Embrace it.

To grow, you must learn, understand and acknowledge the lesson. Everything we go through is meant for our greater good.

"For I know the plans I have for you, says the Lord, plans to prosper you and not to harm you, plans to give you hope and a future" - Jeremiah 29:11.

There is always a bigger picture, even when the tears make it difficult to see it. You must be open to receiving the wisdom from the situation. When the

beauty of it fades, don't allow the pain
of it to consume you.

Wisdom then allows us to forgive the
other person and yourself. Until we are
blessed with our true mate, every
relationship will end. Be mature
enough to let go and allow yourself to
flourish beyond a situation that is over.

Say out loud and with commitment, "The relationship is over".

The relationship is over, YOU are not. I
understand how easy it can be to try to
take full responsibility for its failure. In
the midst of trying to shoulder all of the
blame, you end up internalizing the
flaws of the relationship. Somehow you
start to wonder if it's you, how you
look, how you talk or even how you
love. How could you not, right? You'd
given your all to a relationship, a
person and an ideal and you came out
on the losing end. It's easier to find
flaws in yourself than to admit that the
relationship itself, just wasn't meant to
be. Who you are, what you want and
what you've prayed for is not subject to

a downgrade. You're simply shifting into the right relationship, right partner and right moment. Let this marinate: You don't need to be prettier, thinner, curvier, more this or less that....

You are enough.

For me, the ironic part about the ending of my situation with Julian, is that memories of the beginning flood my mind. Things replay so often and I can clearly see the holes in us and it's so obvious I should have ran for the hills. Julian and I met on a breezy but warm January night where the standard California temperatures provided just enough warmth to both confuse and comfort. The irony that our relationship's theme would later be comfort and confusion, is slightly comical now. I had been back home in California for a while, after two amazing years at college in Florida, when we met at a mutual friend's birthday party. I wasn't at the party looking for anything except an escape from what I was dealing with in private. I would later be told Julian was immediately fixated on me, like "Who is that?!" And I would've been flattered, but I'll admit, I wasn't in the best space when Julian and I met. I had just entered a new relationship at the time and it was already on the rocks. Still, I couldn't lie; I was attracted to him and, in no time, I would find myself more addicted to his presence than I ever cared to admit. The beginning of Julian and I – the comfort and the confusion – would set the tone for the ending of and then, thankfully, the reclamation of my value. But first, I had to admit that I needed healing.

9-27-2014
2:17p

Now, let's begin to heal. It's time to climb out of the hurt and get back to happy.

"Follow your bliss and the universe will open doors where there were only walls" - Joseph Campbell

Focusing on the things/situations/people that are a source of pain brings us more of what we don't want. I recently began writing down things that make me feel good. Every morning I open my journal and title the page "follow your bliss". Then,

I write down a list of things that bring me joy. No matter how small or silly it may seem, it goes on the bliss list. Things like the drive-thru car wash, painting my nails, solo dates to the movie theater and my favorite restaurant, early morning yoga, hugging my nephew, and making a stranger smile are all some of my favorite bliss bringers. Having a bliss list helps me put happiness into perspective. So many times we are caught up in trying to chase, capture and flaunt this idealistic picture of happiness that we forget the small things that easily mount up to the greatest, happiest moments of our lives. I make it a point to do a few things on my bliss list each day. This allows me to constantly remain in a happy space; it keeps me aware of life's "small joys".

I've found that when the focus is bliss, then bliss becomes your reality. Creating a bliss list as a daily exercise is super helpful when coming out of the dark place of heartache. When things seem so tragic and painful, small reminders of happy become slivers of light at the end of the tunnel. As long as you are making a conscious effort to bring a bit of light to a dark moment, darkness can't prevail. Despite how you feel, darkness after heartache cannot win unless you give it permission to. Creating your bliss list is your first step to rejecting the darkness that so easily settles in after a devastating breakup.

It may take baby-steps, but getting back to whole and happy after heartbreak is possible. We don't belong in bitterness and we weren't created for depression. The sooner we clear our minds of the hurt fog, the sooner we can begin thinking joyful thoughts again. Go back to God. God is super creative! This one man and this one relationship isn't the greatest that God has for you. If it was, God would have never allowed it to end. Remember, better is coming. Until then, follow your bliss to your healing.

Start now!

Create your first bliss list below. What amuses you? Who makes you laugh uncontrollably? What makes you feel beautiful? Where do you go to have a good time? What have you been wanting to do but haven't made time for? Write it down.

FOLLOW YOUR BLISS

Poetically Inclined

Who Are You Then?
when you are by yourself ....
far removed from the opinions of others
mistakes you've made, paint your skin
like a mockery of body art.
residue of salt trails streak your face from
tears that have been long dried.
stripped down and bare, no space for secrets
to hide.
who are you then?
with honesty strapped to your chest like a
bullet proof vest
guarding your heart from the facades you
force feed to the world.
who are you then?
does love still ooze from your pores like
overactive sweat glands?
are you gentle with self as you are with the
feelings of "friends"?
are you still you?
is this when you allow yourself to process the
dealings of the days before

take off the layers of lies labeled "I'm okay" "I
love you, TOO"
and the infamous "I am over him"
who are you then?
imperfections on display, do you stare at them
or avert your eyes out of shame?
when forgiveness is the only flaw you really
struggle with...
forgive self.
love self.
learn self.
without the "them" or "him" or the "it"
who are you then?

xo,
McK

To the Queens: who need to trust their intuition

"The only real valuable thing is intuition" - *Albert Einstein*

Although Albert Einstein was considered a genius, learning to trust our intuition is not rocket science. I am convinced that some women don't truly want trust in their relationships. Why? Think about how many of our friends, family members and even ourselves, have made a list of characteristics we desire in a partner. The list may include things like height, kindness, tenacity and even a great relationship with God. While all of these things are awesome, the characteristic of trust should trump all others on the list. Sure, we all want to be able to soundly and easily trust our mates, but how many of us put just as much of a requirement on trusting ourselves?

Queens, it's time to fall back in trust with yourself. As women, we have been gifted with the spirit of knowing. We're all familiar with that persistent feeling in our gut that tells us that something is off with a person or a situation. Sometimes we ignore it and other times we make a mountain of excuses on its behalf. Why? It's either because we're fearful of losing something/someone we value or it's because deep down inside we don't want to believe it to be true. Either way, we must start having enough self-trust to know whether to proceed, take caution or leave. A huge component of trusting our intuition is trusting God.

"Trust in the Lord with all your heart and lean not on your own understanding; in all your ways submit to Him and He will make your paths straight" - Proverbs 3:5.

We must understand that God will never desire our heart to ache or our mind to lack peace. If those things are plaguing us, those are telltale signs of our need to evaluate and change some things about our situation. Trusting God makes it so much easier to trust ourselves. When you trust you, tapping into and adhering to your intuition becomes your nature. Isn't it much better to look back and say, "I dodged that bullet" rather than "I knew I should have listened to my gut"?

"To know and not do is really not to know" - Stephen Covey

There is an art to learning your intuition and it takes a bit of daily practice to become seamlessly in tune with it. Slow down and pay attention to yourself. What other areas of your life are you not listening to yourself? Do you still take the highway when your gut clearly prompted you to take the streets? Paying attention to your gut could have easily helped you avoid that traffic jam on the highway, which made you late for work and began your entire day off on the wrong foot. Start your day by quieting your mind and tuning into God, first. Allow God to be so much a part of your thought process that decisions - the correct and peace providing decisions - become more of a frequent habit.

Daily meditation and affirmations have helped me to become more God guided and trusting. Fifteen minutes of silent meditation before my personal Bible study has been absolutely life changing.

"Meditate on the Word day and night"

Meditation and daily "I AM" affirmations are meant to fuel us with power and belief. The more equipped with peace, faith and confidence we become, the better our conversations with self will be. Day in and day out, the world gives us more than enough opinions and distractions to discredit our own greatness. We have to work overtime to make sure that what we say about ourselves, in the form of daily affirmations, overrides all else. Once we work to cultivate a trust filled relationship with self, built on God, second-guessing will become a thing of the past.

Once internal comfort and confidence has been established, our relationships with men will reflect true trust. We will be more efficient and wise with the time we choose to invest. Gone are the days of stacking up receipts of disappointment while we tirelessly hold on in hopes of something different happening. It's a new day.

Start now!

Be bold and honest with your "I AM" affirmations. Think big, believe big and speak big. Where you write your daily affirmations doesn't matter. I've written them everywhere from journals to bathroom mirrors. The goal is to have the words resonate in your spirit. Choose a place (or places) that will help do that. Here are a few of my favorite affirmations!

"And God said unto Moses, I AM THAT I AM: and He said, Thus shalt thou say unto the children of Israel, I AM hath sent me unto you" - Exodus 3:14

I AM beautiful
I AM worthy
I AM blessed
I AM favored
I AM creative
I AM loved
I AM respected

I AM powerful
I AM awesome
I AM healed
I AM forgiven
I AM safe
I AM a child of God
I AM wealthy
I AM healthy
I AM the shit!!!!
I AM expansive
I AM God guided
I AM chosen
I AM meant for great things
I AM worth it
I AM confident
I AM that…I AM!!

Your turn!

Create affirmations that resonate with you and stir you to believe better about self.

11-23-2012
8:48p

Poetically Inclined

Bottom Line

*I love you
when you piss me off, when you hurt me.
it doesn't fade or go away.
it hangs...
suspended in the air like the lingering of a
favorite fragrance.*

and I love you.

*xo,
McK*

To the Queens: stranded on Desperation Island

No matter how tightly you grip it, how often you turn the other cheek, or the perfection you desire him to have, it will simply not work if the answer is:

He is not the one for you.

Love is the easy part. To have the green light for a relationship to flourish, love can't be the sole determining factor. What about forgiveness, compassion, communication, fun, faith and loyalty? The components for a relationship are the foundation that either makes or breaks it. Think about the process of building a home. You start with a strong foundation and add on elements that make up a house. Whether you choose brick or vinyl siding, the proper application of a foundation determines if a house passes or fails an inspection. If you skimp in any area, the house will undoubtedly fail. Similarly, if you skimp in foundational aspects of a relationship, your relationship will be shaky over time. Your house of love can be overflowing with love, but how long will it stand with a faulty structure?

Looking back, I can now self-diagnose myself with "desperation" from the end of 2011 until…. now! I definitely still have moments of relapse; but now that I'm aware of my diagnosis, I'm able to deal with the feelings and emotions accordingly. Back then, I was plagued by this intense attraction for Julian. If there's one thing I know, it's that there's nothing more dangerous than being addicted to the flesh, bones and flaws of another human being. In fact, it can be quite scary and uncontrollable.

There is one moment that stands out so vividly because it brought it blaring to my attention how deeply attached I had become. It was a Saturday night and I was due to meet up with my friends for a Girl's Night at one of their houses. I lived in Los Angeles at the time, so I was excited to head back to my hometown for some much needed time with friends. On the way out of the city, I ended up stopping by the recording studio Julian was working in for the evening. I stayed for about an hour at the studio, geeked because I was able to steal these little bits of time with him. All the while, I was keeping my friends waiting, knowing I still had to drive over an hour to get to them. When I finally was preparing to leave him, it happened. I went in to kiss him goodbye and he stopped me. "We aren't having sex, kissing isn't a good idea. I will have to take you in one of the studio bathrooms and it'll be a wrap". I was shook. I was desperate. I wanted this kiss so badly and was pleased that he was taking into consideration my choice to abstain from sex at that time. I hopped on the freeway but had to pull over because I was having an anxiety attack. I literally couldn't breathe properly because I was needing this intimacy and feeling neglected. It was overwhelming and scary. Who had I become?

A noticeable symptom of desperation is allowing your heart to be used in a masochist-friendly game of tug-o-war. Your heart was stolen by Mr. Wrong and every few weeks you are in a losing battle of "please baby, baby, please give me my heart back". You remember those old-time cartoons where one character foolishly pulled on a rope while another character, with more strength and a vantage point of their imminent win, pulls from the other end? Loving someone out of desperation is just like that cartoon.

Loving him should never hurt you.

Desperation tends to begin with falling in love with the idea of what could be when the reality of the situation offers no evidence of it even being REAL. We mustn't be so desperate for a companion that we lose ourselves. You were confident in what you wanted before you met them; you shouldn't be willing to sacrifice that for any amount of begging, pleading, sexy glances or romantic gestures. The facts about what a relationship truly is, generally stares us smack-dab in our faces. We have to be willing to be honest about what love is and isn't. I can't urge you enough to give your situation an honest look. Are you happy? Are you fascinated by the idea of him and trying to force a relationship that is nonexistent? If any of your answers came with even an ounce of pause it's time to:

Let it go.

Compromising your morals to get or keep a man never ends well. If having him in your life isn't in line with your faith, your long-term life goals or your journey toward becoming your best self… let it go. We have been created to give and receive love; loving someone does not mean a relationship is meant to happen. It just means you are living God's second greatest commandment of "love thy neighbor as thyself". Settling for a desperate love, only simplifies the great love story that God has in store for you.

8-1-2017

6:20p

Coming into the light of self-love while dealing with heartache, became a far-off reality for me. But it had to happen. Eventually, I had to be released from this hold. That day came. It was the summer of 2016 when Julian came to my house. At that moment, we were on after an off-on-off-on pattern of not speaking. The conversation was light until I mentioned that I had recently met someone. He immediately began to downplay the notion of me finding a great guy by insinuating how flawed my decision-making skills were regarding men. At some point the conversation shifted to him and his so-called feelings toward me.

I'm sitting on my kitchen counter and he's standing about 3 feet in front of me. He's in my space professing his love for me. Boldy. Inconsiderately. A slap in the face to the fact that I just told him I was dating again. All I could do is stare at him with tears in my eyes. Fuming. "How dare you?!" I wanted to scream, slap him or curse him out for playing this game, again. "You decide to love me now?" Really?

But all that I could muster the energy to say was,

"I can't do this".

He left that day with less of my respect. Even with my respect for him dwindling, I couldn't help but wonder when my hope would. After five years of friendship, falling outs, lust, love, anger, hurt, depression and bitterness, there was still this nagging part of me that hoped. I hoped he was telling the truth. I hoped this time our communication would yield peace in our relationship.

I still had hope that he would choose me.

Poetically Inclined

Unrequited
*Gluttonous portions of patience
I overindulge on the frequency of forgiveness
given you.
Eloquent excuses for lack of time, effort, truth,
communication.
No biggie
It's cool.
Whatever makes you happy.*

but what about me?

*xo,
McK*

The most important lesson I learned from desperation is that I created the pattern and flow of the relationship. Often, as women, we forget our power; even worse, we give it away freely. It's both okay to want more from a relationship and to make the decision to leave if you don't get the increase you're desiring. If you allow mediocrity, confusion, mistreatment, and hurt, then the pattern continues.

Be the more that you desire.

Allow me to give you one life lesson that spans across every area of your life: Your words and actions must match. When it comes to relationships, what is the point of saying what you want but accepting everything that you hate? You hate cheaters, liars and men who don't commit; but you take back the cheater, believe the liar and give your loyalty to the man seeking attention and validation from multiple women. This is desperation.

Desperation: an emotional state of despair that typically results in rash or extreme behavior and inappropriate decisions that wouldn't be made in a rational state of mind.

Sound familiar? Pack your bags, get off of the island. Command your mind and heart to line up with God's will because it is painfully obvious what operating out of your own understanding brings to you. Unapologetically accept that you are worthy of exactly what and who you want.

This is a lesson that you will revisit more than once. We will face moments when he comes back - because they always come back - and we must stand strong on FACTS. The facts tell you how he makes you feel, how true he is to his word and, most importantly, how much desperation is included in the recipe of your relationship. Men lie, women lie, facts don't.

He is STILL not the one for you.

But you, Queen, you are STILL worthy of peace, loyalty, laughter, love, respect, affection, communication, comfort, understanding, support, protection and commitment! It matters not how many times he says, "I miss you" and "I love you" if what brings us true joy is missing in the relationship. "I miss you" sounds poetic, but not as poetic if trust is missing. "I love you" makes your heart skip a beat, but it's not as amazing if respect is missing. Stand strong. Let go. Stop answering the calls, stop replying to the messages, stop checking his social media, stop pining away for a make-believe man selling dreams that always manifest as real-life nightmares. Desperation is emotional suicide and we mustn't become a statistic. Choose life.

Start now!

Be honest with yourself. What is so great about the situation you are in? Set a timer for 2 minutes and spend one minute making a list of the pros and one minute making a list of the cons. Does the list of cons outweigh the pros? Was it difficult to think of pros? Are you happy or are you comfortable because you have been on this rollercoaster for so long? Ask yourself this: "Why am I scared to let go of this situation that does not fulfill me?" Allow the truthful answer to penetrate you to your core.

BE HONEST!

PROS

_____

_____

_____

_____

_____

_____

_____

_____

_____

_____

_____

_____

_____

_____

_____

CONS

_____

_____

_____

_____

_____

_____

_____

_____

_____

_____

_____

_____

_____

_____

_____

Poetically Inclined

Survivor

*Don't be that girl who forgets her worth and
misplaces her standards.
Your happiness is not a wallet or set of keys.
Don't be that girl that sacrifices true
happiness
as if happiness is optional.
Make joy mandatory.
Protect your peace and guard your heart…
from unworthy men and more importantly,
from your own bad decisions.
Keep your wits about you Queen.
Desperation is not some mystical land
Desperation is an island much frequented
by women obsessed with finding paradise in a
mirage of a King
who only knows how to desert her.*

*To the Queens,
building rafts out of wisdom and using self-
love to paddle your way to freedom, you are
not Ginger nor Maryann
Desperation Island is no fun.*

It is time to leave.

xo,
McK

To the Queens: who forgot how to love themselves

"Mirror, Mirror on the wall
who's the fairest of them all..."

The evil queen almost had it right. The image in the mirror should be one of the most influential sources of love in your life. She is the one person you must live with forever. Jonathan Butler sings "falling in love with Jesus was the best thing I ever, ever done" and I 100% agree. The moment I truly fell in love with God and His will for my life, my love for self and love for others seemed to explode with growth. How dare I allow mistreatment from anyone, including myself? If you are allowing someone to treat you badly, you have probably dropped the ball on self-love somewhere along the way. You have probably spent hours and hours tearing yourself apart with self-defeating thoughts and constant negative talk. "I can't" and "I'm not" should not precede thoughts about your dreams and self-image. You CAN do whatever your mind conceives. You ARE smart enough, beautiful enough, YOU enough. God is in you and with you.

"I can do all things through Christ who strengthens me" - Philippians 4:13.

Remember that loving and valuing self are included in the "ALL things" part of the scripture above.

1-23-2013
12:58 am

Poetically Inclined

Eden
dare to exist inside of a place
where fear is nonexistent and joy ever present
where the things that should cripple you,
sprout wings and help you soar.
dwell in happiness.
be bound by nothing
where truth, loyalty and honesty
are not luxuries of happenstance
but integral components of one's DNA
dare to love yourself
it may hurt
it may challenge you
but it will be worth it.

xo,
McK

My friends and the women I take on as clients get love- bombed by me often. I frequently send out texts asking them to tell me ten things they love about themselves. I remember the first time I did this, it was shocking and sad to see how many of them could only come up with a few things or, sadly, none at all. What hurt my heart the most was the amount of answers that were only physical attributes.

You have more value than a body could ever offer and you are more beautiful than just your face. Focus on loving what makes you, you; because your body can change and your face will age. The core of you is what matters most.

Take some time to think about what you offer as a person. What are you most proud of? Is it your heart, spirit, mind, tenacity or something even greater? What is it about your character that you love? Notice how good you feel when you have a great hair day or when your eyebrows look amazing or when your makeup is flawless. Those are the moments when you feel like EVERYTHING will go your way.

Well, think of self-confidence and self-love as your spirit having the very best hair day...ever! Feel so good about yourself that you will want to be and do all things that are for you.

Your attitude and confidence dictate how fulfilling your life will be. When you thoroughly love yourself and place high value on your life, mediocrity becomes not only impossible…but frustrating. If at any time you feel so far away from the "you" you once knew- the "you" who was always happy, fearless and willing to trust God; baby step your way back. Do this by affirming daily the things you love about yourself. Even if you start with one thing, build from there. For some, it might be your resiliency and others, it could be your giving heart. Learn to unapologetically beam with pride over what makes you the love of your own life.

Start now!

Revisit our "I AM" affirmations from chapter 2. Add to the list and make it a point to say them twice per day-morning and night. Need help figuring out what you love about yourself? Ask a few of your close friends and family members what they love about you and don't negate the love they offer. Accept it and give them even more of it! Stop comparing yourself to women on social media, in movies, in magazines and on television.

Now, list 10 things you love about yourself. Try to only acknowledge 3 physical characteristics.

1. _____
2. _____
3. _____
4. _____
5. _____
6. _____
7. _____
8. _____
9. _____
10. _____

Poetically Inclined
Am I Enough?

Just knowing I exist, is that enough for you?
Loving me beyond the physical, is that enough
for you?
How can I love you in a way that eliminates
the need for additions…
Be better for you, pure for you, the only one
for you?
Or am I just not what you need at this
moment?
Will you ever love me outside of selfishness
and in the space of real
because I need more.
I need to have the right to be angry and
demand all of you.
the security of knowing I am all you desire.
The status of being yours. undeniably.
the risk of throwing caution to the wind and
us just trying
we will never know if we never begin
I want to start being your only one
is that enough for you?
xo,
McK

<u>To the Queens: who are ready to move on</u>

I'm no expert on love, but I am well versed in hurt. I have learned that the moment you are on one accord (mentally, emotionally and spiritually) with your desire to feel better, you will. Facing fear, which tends to be the main reason we remain stuck in hurt, should be the first thing you confront. Have you ever stood face-to-face with someone who looked way taller/larger/frightening in picture, only to see that they weren't as large as your mind made you believe they were? That's exactly the facing you have to do when it comes to fear. Face the fear of being alone. Face the fear of failure (remember: the relationship failed, YOU ARE NOT A FAILURE). Face the fear of the unknown. It can certainly be scary to leave a comfort zone, especially when you have no clue what comes next. I had to constantly remind myself:

"be strong and courageous! Do not be afraid or discouraged, for the Lord your God is with you wherever you go" -Joshua 1:9.

I reasoned that whatever was coming had to be better than the pain. WRONG! Leaving this love hurt so badly because I hadn't realized my addiction to him rivaled that of a drug addict. Just like a drug habit, the withdrawal phase was brutal. I tried everything. It all worked. I had to be consistent in my efforts to move on. This wasn't a two-week task. I made lists of reasons why I had to leave, I erased and blocked his number on all devices, I deleted him from social media sites, I erased pictures and old texts. I prayed, I fasted, I dated other people, I focused on my health and fitness. I cried, I screamed, I read and listened to personal development books. And I wrote this book you're currently reading. Constantly. The last time I was intimate with him was over a year ago and I still do a lot of these "moving on mechanisms" to keep me on the straight and narrow. In the beginning of 2013, I was introduced to the book The Four Agreements and I am pretty sure it saved my life.

1. be impeccable with your word
2. don't take anything personally
3. never assume
4. always do your best

It was the second agreement, don't take anything personally, that helped me to mentally shift in such a huge way. When I stopped blaming him for my anger and bitterness, it empowered me to release myself from the victim role and reclaim my value. I then understood that what I received from him was a reflection of how he felt about himself; it wasn't a "Mia issue" that I had to hold on to. I stopped accepting the baggage of terrible treatment when I became determined not to take his inability to not be what I needed, wanted or deserved – personally. A lot of times, we want someone to blame for the mistreatment we receive from others. Sometimes we blame circumstances and other times we blame ourselves. Please remember: when someone treats us with or without kindness, it is directly correlated to their own love and value of self.

That was my "ah ha" moment. I was no longer mean and cold. I continued to work on myself and continued to find my lessons I needed to learn while learning to forgive both myself and him simultaneously. There will be moments when you backslide… simply refocus on forgiving more and get right back to moving on.

"examine yourselves as to whether you are in faith. test yourselves" 2 Corinthians 13:5

After not seeing him for nine months and only having brief conversations… I recently spent some time with him. I needed to. I wanted to be sure the residue of him was gone. I hugged him for a very long time, and for the first time in years, I felt nothing. At first, it was scary and finally, it settled in my spirit as being extremely refreshing. The hold had been broken. The whole Mia had returned. I can wish him the best in life and be at total peace with having no ties and no communication with him. As terrifying as moving on has been, it has also been the most rewarding growth opportunity. I never thought I would see this day and that was the problem back then. I focused on failure thoughts and became my freedom's worst enemy. It took changing and reprogramming my mind to essentially change my life.

Step 1: release the fear of the unknown that comes with releasing love.
Step 2: forgive. forgive. forgive. forgive some more. and forgive again
Step 3: do these things and read this pocket guide as often as needed.

Start now!

9-8-2014

5:00p

Poetically Inclined

Free

I have been waiting for the day when
certain numbers, words, places and scents
no longer reminded me of you.
I was wondering when love would untwine
with our past.
couldn't wait for this moment when your
name
wouldn't actually cause physical pain…
and a clock would just be a clock
not a countdown until the next time
I felt you...had you...welcomed you in
me.

feels amazing to be free
finally.

xo,
McK

closing remarks

It hasn't been an easy road, getting to this place of complete love of self. A few pit stops were made along the way. Needing to be enough for him, wanting to be enough for him. Hurting because I didn't understand me being me wasn't enough for him to choose only me. Wasn't I loyal enough? Wasn't I available enough?

I kept trying to change me to fit with him and the results were world shattering. I had to do something differently because my frustration with this failing situation was seeping into every area of my life. I became angry, cold, bitter, mean and jealous. The worst part? I didn't know how to stop it. It was like making a wrong turn or missing your exit on the highway. I kept going thinking I could eventually get back on the correct route. But the more wrong turns and the more I ignored my GPS (intuition), I ended up so far away from my destination....so far from ME that it was scary! I can remember driving down the freeway, crying out to God and asking Him to forgive me. How dare I allow anyone treat me this way? Treat me as if I wasn't purposefully, hand crafted by the ultimate creator. I was embarrassed, ashamed and ready to be who God created me to be.

"it's not about what you walk away from, it's about what you walk away with" - Lil Wayne

He wasn't the issue anymore, it was me. I had to remove myself from him so that I could get ME back. As cliché as it may sound, time is definitely the best doctor. I didn't fall for him overnight and I wasn't healed of his presence overnight either. . It was a process….it IS a process… that requires constant personal development and brutal honesty with myself. Be honest with yourself that getting over someone who impacted your heart and life so much, will take time. I took him out of my life equation months ago and NOW, dang near four years since our first kiss, I am able to see that my self-destruction didn't even start with him. As with any major life decision, it started and ended with me. I chose to love out of desperation. I chose to make myself available to someone who was unavailable to me. I chose to be someone's all when I could barely get part-time reciprocity. I made all of those choices because I wasn't in tune and in love with myself. The truth was, I didn't know myself enough to love anyone!

The men before Julian weren't to blame either. I understand that these experiences were needed for me to get to this place. Some decisions regarding men are still difficult to make, but I know how to operate from a place of high self-worth. I make it a point to connect and communicate with women who feed the Queen in me.

8-1-2017

6:20p

2016 brought me to this interesting space of being healed. Only in the sense that I wasn't crying my eyes out. I was no longer angry or bitter. I felt good.

But my ego.

My ego was shattered by this man. I literally had to handle myself with care every single time we had interactions. Why was I so pressed to be chosen by him? What was this sick control over me he possessed? At times, I recalled feeling like a robot – knowing what was happening, but waiting on the person with the control to make the moves for me. I wasn't living up to the me that had met him on a warm night in California. It was almost as if I was watching a movie on fast-forward and watched myself disappear and be replaced with a more diluted version of myself. Still, sometimes your ego has to shock you out of the dilution you've sunk yourself into.

A few weeks after the kitchen convo, I texted him and let him know that it would be best if we didn't communicate. On my end, the guy I was dating triggered something different in me. I wanted to explore that without distractions. Not that Julian and I were discussing being together, it was just that it became clear to me that my "hope addiction" needed to be broken.

What am I hoping for?

The answer took so many disappointments, tears, desperation, years and lies to figure out.

It was never him.

It was always me.

I was hoping to be chosen because I never committed to choosing myself. In friendships, in school, in too many life decisions I thought of others first instead of myself. I was infatuated with his lies, hoping my feelings for him would turn them into truths. This only left me open to neglect my own truth. I kept hoping each time we were on speaking terms, that the outcome would be different. Because I was different. I was better. I saw that; I knew he'd have to see that.

In all my growth, forgiveness and healing, I forgot to release my grip on him. As much of a space filler he was in my life, I realized I was the same thing in his. Neither of us were doing anything to push the either forward or further. We were just existing amongst the complexed, twisted and confused interaction we occasionally called a situationship. We were just filling time in each other's lives and my desperation hung onto the hope that it would magically create something from nothing. It wouldn't. It couldn't. You see, he was to my life what the bully in school was to the picked on kid: A lesson that didn't need revisiting or cordial interaction.

Imagine having the ultimate glow up in life and going back to the hood to show off. It isn't necessary. The hood can be very unforgiving. Going back to the place of pain can taint the beauty of who you became because of it. How many stories have been heard about stars being called "too Hollywood" by their hometown homies? How many stories tell the tale of haters in the hood trying to bring down those who made it out? Don't we all know of instances where the people closest to us are the last to support?

This is what I realized had been happening every time he and I would become cordial again. He supported or congratulated me only according to what he deemed important. He would say things like how predictable my dating life was and how he learned to let me make mistakes and bad decisions. It was like he expected and wanted every relationship of mine to fail.

We were on Facetime during my lunch break one day and I suggested we go on a date. He was shook. No more eye contact and a flood of excuses came. He claimed that I wasn't ready for what he was looking for. He rejected me by using me as a scapegoat. He couldn't just say no. It was like he HAD to make it my fault even though it was me who suggested we try our hand at seriously dating. It was then that I finally seen how manipulative he was.

Soon after that conversation, his Instagram boasted pictures of him on dates and bae-cations with his so-called ex-girlfriend.

I laughed as I blocked his number,

email address and all social media accounts.

My hope died when I finally understood how much we both needed to be out of each other's lives. My hope stopped hurting me when I let go of trying to prove I was good enough, evolved enough, loving enough. There is no way to be enough for someone who you are only meant to learn from not progress with.

Five years later, I am completely over that heartbreak and beyond capable of conquering any additional heartache that may come my way. Learning to love myself seriously gave me super powers.

I have the power to forge ahead regardless of what relationship I am in or out of. I have the power to choose myself no matter who doesn't. I have the power to heal, forgive and let go knowing none of these makes me a less loyal girlfriend. Letting go of hurt and misdirected hope have proven to be the key to changing my story. They are the reset buttons for my heart. Ironically, the very hurt and hope that I clung to, as if my life depended on it, turned out to be the very things that allowed me to receive more. Releasing that hurt and hope opened the windows and doors for all of the blessings waiting with my name on it. The only way I could've unlocked them, though? Letting go of the unnecessary pain that I'd started to become bosom buddies with.

Being able to receive more love, growth, peace and having the freedom to walk in my worth, is the gift that keeps on giving. It's the gift that, unknowingly, I was searching for in every one of my past desperation-based relationships. I was on the hunt for something that lies, betrayal, low-self-worth and insecurity could never seem to give me.

Growing into the new me (who is still growing, by the way) helps me to proudly showcase my superpowers. Every day I choose the power to operate as my very best self. I own the power to place more value on choosing myself rather than desiring men to choose me.

I am free from needing validation and I am fully enrolled in the forever journey of self-love.

The continuous seeking of God allows me to stand firm on His promises and be open to learning lessons, receiving love and trusting His timing on everything. I truly pray that something in this pocket guide becomes rooted in you and ignites your courage to let go of situations and people that tarnish your crown.

Thank you for allowing me to share. Thank you for rolling with me on this journey to healing, self-love and obedience to God. I will forever welcome LIFE and all of the things we tend to experience, if that means overcoming it will serve as an inspiration for you to do the same.

I love all of me so that I am able to give this same love ….

to the queens.
xo,
MiaMcK

www.ingramcontent.com/pod-product-compliance
Lightning Source LLC
LaVergne TN
LVHW051430080426
835508LV00022B/3323